American Indians

THE NAVAJO

by N.C. Barnes

DiscoverRoo
An Imprint of Pop!
popbooksonline.com

WELCOME TO DiscoverRoo!

This book is filled with videos, puzzles, games, and more! Scan the QR codes* while you read, or visit the website below to make this book pop.

popbooksonline.com/Navajo

abdobooks.com

Published by Pop!, a division of ABDO, PO Box 398166, Minneapolis, Minnesota 55439.

Printed in the United States of America, North Mankato, Minnesota.

052024
082024

THIS BOOK CONTAINS RECYCLED MATERIALS

Cover Photo: Julien McRoberts/Danita Delimont Photography/Newscom
Interior Photos: Getty Images, Shutterstock Images, Wikimedia
Editor: Emily Dreher
Series Designer: Colleen McLaren

Library of Congress Control Number: 2023947593

Publisher's Cataloging-in-Publication Data

Names: Barnes, N.C., author.
Title: The Navajo / by N.C. Barnes
Description: Minneapolis, Minnesota : Pop!, 2025 | Series: American Indians | Includes online resources and index
Identifiers: ISBN 9781098246228 (lib. bdg.) | ISBN 9781098246785 (ebook)
Subjects: LCSH: Navajo Indians--Juvenile literature. | American Indians--Juvenile literature. | Indians of North America--Juvenile literature. | Indigenous peoples--Social life and customs--Juvenile literature. | Cultural anthropology--Juvenile literature.
Classification: DDC 973.0497--dc23

*Scanning QR codes requires a web-enabled smart device with a QR code reader app and a camera.

TABLE OF CONTENTS

CHAPTER 1

WHO ARE THE NAVAJO?

Before European **settlers** came to North America, the land was mostly wild and open. It was populated by American Indians. Each group had its own languages and culture. Culture is the customs, arts, and ideas of a group of people.

WATCH A VIDEO HERE!

The Navajo Nation is one of the most well-known American Indian groups.

The Navajo refer to themselves as *Diné*. It means "the people" in the Navajo language. The Navajo originally lived in what is now Canada. Between 1100 and 1500 CE they traveled south. Most made their home in Utah, New Mexico, and Arizona.

NAVAJO HOMELANDS

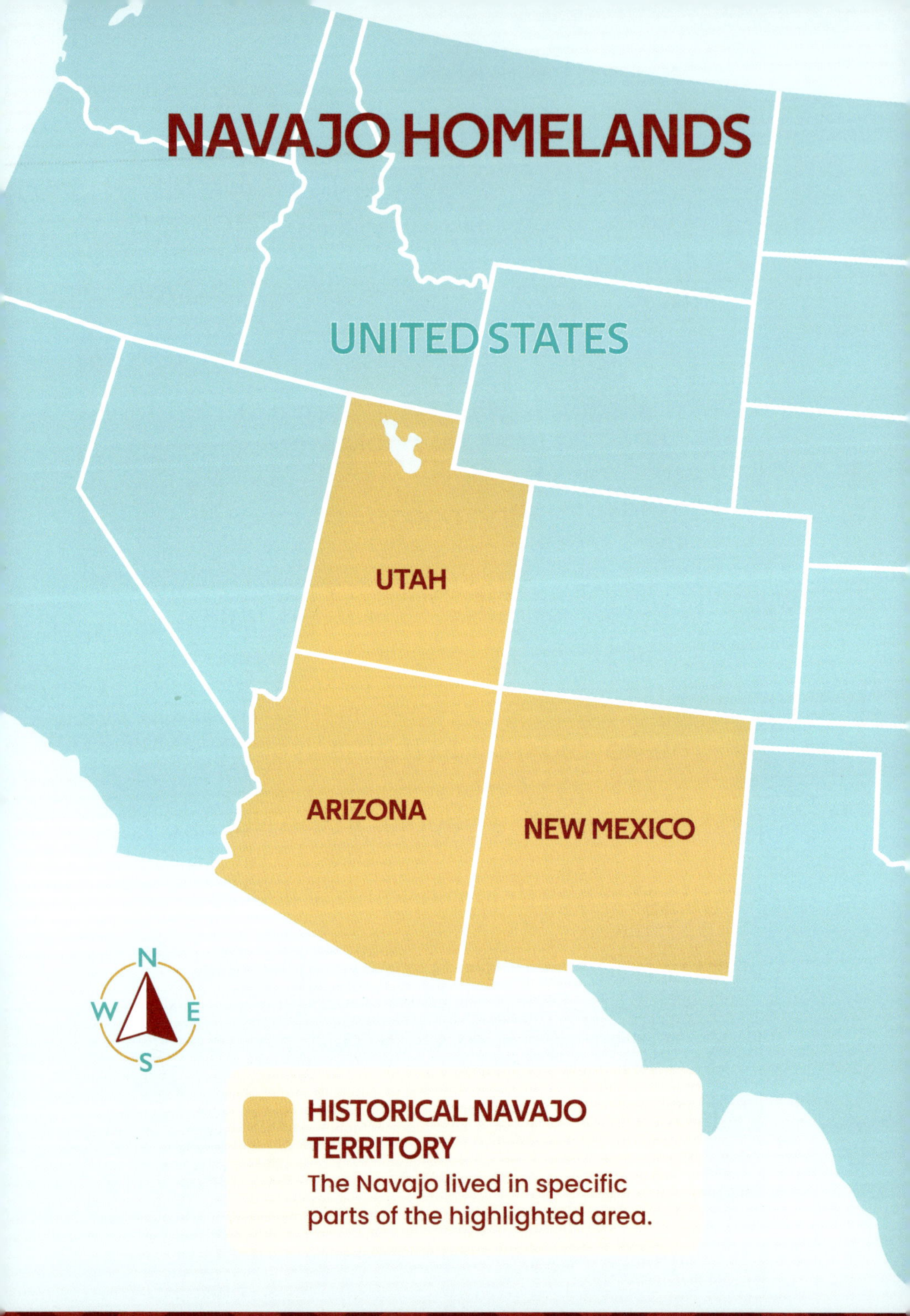

HISTORICAL NAVAJO TERRITORY

The Navajo lived in specific parts of the highlighted area.

DID YOU KNOW?

There are four mountains, four seasons, four cardinal directions, and a Navajo person's four clans.

Navajoland or *Diné Bikéyah* is set between four **sacred** mountains. They are Mount Blanca to the east, Mount Taylor to the south, San Francisco Peak to the west, and Mount Hesperus to the north. Four is an important number to the Navajo people.

Navajoland has canyons and rock formations.

Navajo people live with a few related families in a group called a clan. Clan membership is passed down through mothers. A Navajo person is connected to four clans. The first clan is their mother's, the second is their father's, and finally the clans of both their grandfathers.

Babies were carried on their mother's back in a cradleboard.

The Navajo lived near the Pueblo, Hopi, and Apache peoples.

Historically, clans lived far apart. They cared for themselves. Navajo clans didn't have specific leaders, but women were usually the decision-makers. They often made decisions based on agreement between clan members.

CHAPTER 2

HISTORICAL LIFE

The Navajo started out as hunters and gatherers. Their land had deserts, canyons, mountains, and forests. The Pueblo people taught the Navajo how to farm the dry land. Once they learned how to farm, life became simpler.

LEARN MORE HERE!

Corn was used to make tortillas.

DID YOU KNOW?

Herbs and spices were used for **ceremonies**.

The Navajo farmed, hunted, gathered, and raised their food. The people grew corn, wheat, vegetables, and melons during the summer. They raised sheep

Navajo people gently sheared their sheep. It did not cause harm.

and goats for their meat, milk, and fur. They gathered prickly pears, peaches, nuts, herbs, and spices from the land around them. Meals were often stew and tortillas.

Diné lived in homes called hogans. Hogans were dome-shaped buildings built with mud, logs, and rocks. The materials and shape of the home kept it cool. Hogans had one door that faced south so the Navajo could wake to the rising sun. They believe the sun gives them blessings.

There was a hole in a hogan's roof to release smoke from a fire.

A shade shelter is called a chaha'oh *in the Navajo language.*

The Navajo spent much of their time outdoors. Shade shelters were built around hogans to protect people from the strong sun. Navajo people worked beneath the shelters. They made food, blankets, clothes, home goods, and art in the shade.

CHAPTER 3

FAMILY AND TRADITIONS

The Navajo were connected through their mothers. They lived in clans of a few families. Diné married outside their clans. The man would move to the woman's village. Usually, a married couple built their home near the bride's mother. All belongings, including **livestock**, were owned by women.

EXPLORE LINKS HERE!

It takes many steps for wool from sheep to become thread to make blankets.

Children took their mother's clan name. Older children cared for younger ones. They learned from adults in their clan. Mothers and aunts handed out chores to the children. Five-year-olds carried water from streams. Older children helped cook and chop wood. All children learned to care for livestock and ride horses.

The Navajo kept Churro sheep. Their coats are longer than other sheep.

Diné weave patterns that represent balance and harmony.

Diné were known for their beautiful art. Women wove rugs and blankets with wool from their sheep. They made dyes for wool out of native plants and **minerals**. Men made jewelry from silver and precious stones.

DID YOU KNOW?

Diné women are known as the best weavers in the world.

Wild horses roamed some of Navajoland.

Before the Navajo started raising sheep, they wore clothes made of deerskin. Eventually, men and women wore beautiful wool blankets as shirts and dresses. These clothes were much cooler than deerskin. They used belts to keep blankets in place.

Diné were very **spiritual** people. They believe in Holy People who can help and harm Earth People. Earth People are humans. They have a responsibility to care for Mother Earth and keep the natural world balanced. Medicine people were spiritual leaders in clans. They were very educated in plants and their uses. They also led **ceremonies**.

HEALING CEREMONIES

The Navajo believed illness was caused by disorder in the **universe**. Medicine people used healing ceremonies to help a sick person get better. During some ceremonies, the sick person sat on a sand painting. The medicine person sang healing songs and asked for good energy to draw illness out of the sick person.

The Navajo believe turquoise is a sacred stone.

CHAPTER 4

AFTER THE EUROPEANS

In the 1600s, the Navajo encountered Spanish explorers. They got sheep and horses from the Spanish. This made travel easier and keeping **livestock** possible. But the nearby Apache nation and the Spanish were enemies. In the 1680s, the Navajo teamed up with the Apache and Pueblo nations to fight the Spanish.

COMPLETE AN ACTIVITY HERE!

Owning a lot of livestock was a sign of high social status.

In the 1800s, Navajoland was traded from the Mexicans to Americans. The Navajo had to negotiate with the US government for rights to their own land and water. Diné often had to fight Americans trying to invade their land.

Young Navajo were sometime sent to US military forts.

The actions of US troops went against how Navajo believe humans should treat the land.

In 1863, the US started forcibly removing Navajo people from their homeland. US troops arrested 8,000 Diné and burned farm fields and livestock. They destroyed water sources. The Navajo were forced to walk 300 miles (483km) to a **reservation** in New Mexico. About 2,000 Navajo members died on the march that became known as the Long Walk.

The Navajo fought to return to their homeland. In 1868, Diné signed a **treaty** with the US government that allowed them to return to their homeland. Today, the Navajo nation has the largest American Indian reservation in the US.

People who work with silver are called silversmiths.

This photo is a re-enactment of the 1868 treaty signing.

DID YOU KNOW?

Mexicans taught Navajo how to make silver jewelry.

The clothing American Indian dancers wear is call regalia.

Some 300,000 Navajo nation members live on a reservation in parts of New Mexico, Arizona, and Utah. As climate patterns have changed over the centuries, Navajoland cannot support all the Diné. Today, Navajo are fighting for access to clean water and healthy food. The Diné are resilient and will not give up fighting for a good life for all its members.

Navajo people have served bravely in the US military.

MAKING CONNECTIONS

TEXT-TO-SELF

The Navajo people spend a lot of time outside with their clans. Do you ever spend time with friends and family outside? Do you enjoy it? What do you do outside?

TEXT-TO-TEXT

Have you read another book about an American Indian nation? How is their culture similar to or different from the Navajo people?

TEXT-TO-WORLD

In the 1800s, the Navajo were forced from their homeland. Can you think of any other groups of people who were forced from their homes? Did they get to go back like some Navajo did?

GLOSSARY

ceremony — a formal event held on a special occasion.

livestock — animals kept or raised for food or resources.

minerals — a nonliving solid with a specific chemical makeup that occurs naturally.

reservation — a piece of land set aside by the government for American Indians to live on.

sacred — something worthy of intense honor.

settler — a person who moves with a group of others to live in a new country or area. A place where settlers live is called a settlement.

spiritual — having to do with people's beliefs in things, such as the soul, nature, and what happens after death.

treaty — a formal agreement.

universe — all existing things, including Earth and the heavens.

INDEX